Adrift

by Gary Rainford

North Country Press
Unity, Maine

Adrift

ISBN 978-1-943424-72-6

LCCN 2022934420

for my mother, who was afraid to live,
who was afraid to die,
and for my wife and daughter, who lead me to water

Acknowledgments

Thank you to the editors at *Aurorean, Café Review, Ibbetson Street Press, Mount Desert Islander, Muddy River Poetry Review,* and *Pensive: A Global Journal of Spirituality and the Arts* where poems in this collection, or earlier versions, originally appeared.

PREFACE

We lose keys. We lose wallets. We lose cellphones. We lose remote controls. We lose our glasses. We lose notes we specifically write to remind us of important tasks. We lose names of people and places on the tips of our tongues. We lose fleeting thoughts, ideas so brilliant and original, if we could have only held on to them. And some of us lose our minds.

According to the Alzheimer's Association, 12.7 million people will be diagnosed with dementia by 2050. This is several million people greater than the population of New York City. Picture America's largest city as an assisted living facility. A demented population confined and roaming all five boroughs with a revolving-door-army of healthcare workers changing adult diapers. Dispensing medications. Picture the Statue of Liberty toddling in circles, weeping, lost in the malignant brain-fog rising out of New York Harbor.

In 2021, the FDA approved Aducanumab, the first-of-its-kind treatment for Alzheimer's disease. Aducanumab is an antibody drug that treats the underlying biology of Alzheimer's, not just common symptoms like memory loss, confusion, obsessive compulsive behaviors and depression. If dementia were a drunk driving accident, Aducanumab is the good sense not to take that first drink in the first place, not the EMTs on-scene, splinting broken bones and patching up bloody gashes. Aducanumab reduces the buildup of Amyloid beta, the plaques found in the brains of people with Alzheimer's.

Hope is on its way even though Aducanumab was not available for Bobbi, my mother, when she was diagnosed with Alzheimer's disease. Too ashamed and stubborn, Bobbi never wanted to talk about dementia, so we pretended it didn't exist when she lost her keys, when she lost her wallet, when she lost her cellphone, when she lost the television remote control, when she lost reminder-notes scattered around her home. When nothing made sense, and I was no longer her son.

Dementia kills in time-lapse. Days, weeks, years, a lifetime passes compressed into minutes. Sometimes seconds. Like traffic slowing down to ogle a car wreck or some other highway catastrophe, these poems are the final stories of my mother's biological head-on collision with the final, time-distorted years of her life.

The 1968 film, *2001: A Space Odyssey*, loops in my head now for every demented, lost cause, the scene where Hal 9000's artificial (yet sentient) intelligence systems are being shut down by Dave, mission commander and sole survivor aboard the spaceship, *Discovery*. Hal says in a calm, soft voice, in contrast to his grim reality, "I'm afraid. I'm afraid, Dave. Dave, my mind is going. I can feel it. I can feel it. My mind is going. There is no question about it. I can feel it. I can feel it. I can feel it. I'm a . . . fraid."

Gary Rainford, Swan's Island, 2021

Adrift adrift
on the sound of rain
on a windless sea
in a sailless skiff

> —Ursula K. Le Guin,
> from *So Far So Good*,
> final poems: 2014-2018

Table of Contents

Reincarnation

"I remember this place," says Bobbi,
exploring the tree-line from a rocking chair
outside Winterberry Heights

and watching the birds. "You've been here
before, Mom?" I say. "Oh sure, I used to come
all the time," Bobbi's eyes are dreamlets,

that borderland, not quite awake, not quite
asleep: tranced and peaceful. Don't argue, I
tell myself. Let her be wherever

she thinks here is. Who knows, says my
brother when I tell him about my visit. Maybe
Mom, in another life, was a bird.

I: ASSISTED LIVING

Where the Heart Is

"If I need you to pick
me up today, you can't,
right?" "Right, Mom.

I'll be back Tuesday."
"Okay, so if I go outside
and find somebody to

take me," Bobbi sniffles
into the phone, then sobs,
"which way is home?"

3

Souvenir Shopping

"I'm not me again," Bobbi sobs
into to the phone, the title sequence
of *The Big Valley*, a 1960's

Western TV series, staring Barbara
Stanwyck and Lee Majors rerunning
in the background. "My mother

named me Barbara because she
loved Barbara Stanwyck." "I didn't
know that, Mom. Tell me more."

Destination Trouble

"My mother needs me,"
I say to Heather, the resident
assistant staffing the front
desk today, Bobbi

and I heading downtown
to Bangor for coffee and kicks.
"We have people to piss
off," Bobbi smirks.

Path of Least Resistance

Google Maps sends us into historic
Queen City Bangor, left on Congress,
left on Broadway, then another left

on Stillwater. "Look at that," Bobbi
says pointing down a dead-end. "What?"
I ask. "A monkey ran across the road,"

she nods. "I've never seen a monkey
do that before." "It's rare," I reply, not
looking for conflict, trying to accept.

Memory Care

Panicked and out of breath she says,
"Do you know 201, Winterberry Heights?
Can you take me home soon?" "Mom,

Winterberry is home." "No, you don't
understand. This is not home. I don't know
how I got here. I don't know where I am;

or anybody. I can't stop shaking. And
my brain doesn't work, doesn't know what
it knows." "Breathe, Mom. Take deep

breaths." "I need a basket for my Maxie
so he can be with me on the stationary bike
in the rec room. All I do is move, move,

move." "That's better than not moving,"
I joke. "I think I'm going to lie down. We
can hang up. I don't have anything else

really to say. Thank you for all you're
doing for me." "I love you, Mom. I'm sorry."
"Maxie sleeps in my arms, but he's half

hiding under the bed now. He dances for
my new friends. I really enjoy the bowls of
dried fruit here. Let's get together soon."

Golden Girl

"You're her son, aren't you?" says Carol
sitting on the garden bench next to Bobbi and me.
A hot July wind sweeps the parking lot

at Winterberry. "Yes, I'm her favorite son,"
I reply playing along. "And don't forget handsome,"
Carol giggles, then blushes candy-apple

lipstick and the sparkly eyes of a dark haired
Betty White. "Let's go now," she tugs Justin's leash,
a corgi-chihuahua mix wearing a pinstriped Polo.

Dyschronometria

"Okay, so it's 6:34," Bobbi says
to herself sitting in the passenger seat.
"That's the time, right?" she asks,

reaches out her fingers for the clock
on the dashboard, as if time were not
a concept, but tangible. "Another

Tuesday night in July," I turn into
Hobby Lobby. "It can't be night. I just
got up." Bobbi scans the parking

lot, clouds in her eyes. "Why do
you do that to me!" she spits. "Mom,
it's not morning. Serious."

Birth Certificate Blues

"Some stupid hospital called asking
about, Jerry," Bobbi's voice cracks like
parchment. "When I try ringing his

cellphone," she continues, "you can't
leave a message. I'm worried. I always
worry about your brother. Since he

was a baby." As parents, we want our
children to grow up healthy, productive
citizens of a kinder, gentler world,

yet deep down we know sorrow runs
amok in every family. "Let me get back
to you later, I can't think now," Bobbi

sighs. But she forgets things once we
say goodbye, the Alzheimer's, the ship-
worms tunneling deeper and deeper.

Quality of a Life

"I'm scared, honey," Bobbi whispers
into the phone, voice quivery as a warbler's
call. "There's nobody around, and I can't
put on my pants. Can you help me?
Can you?"

Aging in Place

Caught off guard Mary smiles,
stops midstride upstairs in the hallway,
then sets the rollator brakes;

the blow-dryer buzzing of Elene's
beauty spa tells the story of shampoo,
cut, color, and permanent waves.

"Your hairdo looks nice," says
Bobbi, running fingers through hers,
thin, wispy, white, out of control.

"Elene is so sweet; and a miracle
worker," Mary's voice, like kindling,
ignites. "She gives me style."

"My son," Bobbi twists a stray
wisp, "says all I do is show up and let
Elene take care of the rest."

"Oh, yes," replies Mary, unhitching
the rollator brakes, leaning into a shuffle.
"Isn't that nice. We are so lucky."

Snapshot in the Family Album

As if she has run a marathon, Bobbi gasps,
"You've got to come get me. I need your help,
I can't stay here." "Mom, I spent all day

with you," I sigh. "I can't drive back now."
"Then when?" she spits venom, all the anger
in the world, all the politics on Facebook;

every natural disaster—hurricanes, tornados,
heatwaves, droughts, pandemics. "Wednesday,
Mom," I remind her knowing her brain is

cracked, a container of sour milk, of people
and places spilling out fast as pouring. "I can't
stay here that long. I'm leaving!" Bobbi's

outrage knocks the wedding picture of her
parents off the windowsill. "Leaving where?"
I ask, but I'm ten years old now, not fifty,

not my mother's legal guardian or her power
of attorney, Incredible Hulk knapsack bungeed
to my Schwinn—adrift, I am running away

from home. I have had enough: my brothers'
fighting, elbows and knees and holes in the walls.
Enough: weekends at my dad's with his new

wife. Enough: my stepfather's ashy, stinking
cigars. Enough. Enough. "Just let me be," Bobbi
half thunders, half sobs, then slams the phone.

Hostility

"Do you have my son's phone number?"
Bobbi asks Lynn, the overnight, front desk
aide. "Oh, honey," she smiles, "it's late

to call your son." "You say that like I ask
all the time," Bobbi replies, arms folded across
her chest, insulted. The heating system hums

up in the ceiling. The ornate dining room
chandeliers shed sleepy shadows on the tables
of empty water glasses and starched, white

tablecloths. Four o'clock in the morning
at Winterberry Heights is quiet, a confused,
muddled place. "Honey," Lynn's voice

is kind, but tired, "you've asked four times
tonight." "Well," Bobbi spits, eyes red peppers,
"you can shove that up your ass! And die!"

Family Tree

"How old is your son?" says Bobbi licking
globs of Boston Kreme donut off gnarled, arthritic
knuckles. "My daughter's name is Meri. I don't

have a son." "That's right, she's one sweet girl."
"Meri rhymes with ear; it's a good way to remember
her name." "Who are you?" Bobbi tugs her earlobe

and says her granddaughter's name. "I'm your son,"
I reply. "That's what you are," Bobbi taps the Pepsi bottle
cap indicating how she wants me to open and pour it

into the box of Dunkin' Donuts. "My daughter,
your granddaughter, *who's afraid of you* (but I don't
say that) is going on twelve in February."

Mysteries

"Your mother called
this morning, upset," I say
to my brother,

Scott. "She says she
thinks about Gram and Pop.
Questions if they are

alive or not. She sees
them. Not just in her mind.
In the apartment too."

Motherhood at Eighty

"Boiling eggs for Max, an entire dozen,
so I couldn't get to the phone fast enough,"
replies Bobbi. "My Max," she continues,

"goes crazy for eggs, hardboiled; I mix
the pieces together, chunky, like egg salad,
and that smarty noses-out all the whites

and wolfs just the yellow crumbs; I swear,
this dog is sharp; you can laugh if you want,
but I love my Max more than you kids."

Sighting

Wrapped inside a napkin inside a lavender
scented poop bag inside a sock stuffed under
three sweatshirts and an empty Nike

sneaker box in the back of her closet is the
steady beep of the wireless keyfinder attached
to Bobbi's keyring. "Found them!" I say

and Bobbi steps into the closet. "These,"
I hold up the keys and push the remote again,
the keyfinder beeping in my hand. "I don't

know who put them there," Bobbi looks like
she spotted Bigfoot. "Maybe it was Bigfoot," I
smile and slip them into her empty pocket.

Chief of the Angels

"Coming, Hun!" shouts Bobbi who scoops up Max
barking at the door. Shaped like an apostrophe Ed is standing
stooped in the hallway. "What day is today?" he asks,

flashing a cartoon smile. "I don't know," Bobbi replies,
then looks at me. "Thursday," I answer appraising the crucifix—
shoelaces wrapped around twigs and big as a hood

ornament—dangling from Ed's neck. "I thought today
was Sunday." Ed grabs the cross with a shaky fist and beams,
"I pray to St. Michael, mostly for mercy. Do you pray?"

Everything in its Place

I check the microwave for Bobbi's keys; I check
the cupboards for laundry; I check the refrigerator
for magazines; I check the couch cushions for
peppermint striped candies; I check inside

the toilet tank for cans of Bush's baked beans;
I check the shower for empty Boost bottles; I check
under the mattress for dirty dishes; I check behind
the window treatments for Max's leash; I

check the TV remote, replace batteries; checking
the closet, I plunge my hands into a case of Depends,
and ask, "Mom, what's the deal?" "Oh, those are
probably used. Once, at least," she replies.

Sundowning

"Gary? I thought you were coming
today," Bobbi's voice strains against
the darkness. "Go back to bed,

Mom," I say into the phone. "It's early,
not time to be awake yet." "But I've been
waiting all day. You never came like

you said. And now it's night." "No,
it's two in the morning, Mom. I will be
there for lunch. I'm bringing soup."

Asian Palace

Bobbi wishbones a fortune cookie;
jagged pieces fly

into my leftover shrimp
egg foo young. "The greatest medicine

is the emptiness of everything,"
she reads aloud,

shakes her head, and asks if I know
what it means.

"Basically," I reply, "it's the concept,
Less is more

on spiritual steroids; it suggests nirvana,
how emptiness is beyond

the world of form, a state of freedom
from stuff, all the extras

we surround ourselves with thinking
they make our lives better,

richer: smartphones, Instagram, Netflix
Originals, even Google . . .

"That's a load of horseshit!"
Bobbi whinnies, 81 years of experience

embellishing every wrinkled line
notched in her face.

Ash Wednesday

"Are you Catholic?" asks a woman
canvasing door-to-door and cradling a
porcelain faith vessel of palm ashes,

dirt from which God made us and dirt
from which we will return. "Ah, hmm, yes,"
Bobbi stammers. "But I'm not as good

as I should be," she adds, no humor
in her voice, no apology either, or regret.
"Do you want to see a priest?" "No,

I'm not ready for that!" Bobbi puts up
her hand, bombshelled by the invocation,
and she can't bolt the door fast enough.

Courtesy Call

"Gary, this is Kelly
from Winterberry; it's

not an emergency;
give me a call when

you get this message,
please; the nurse

is trying to remove
your mother's stitches,

but she won't sit still
long enough to let us

near her pinkie; even
with me holding her

other hand she's upset
about *real* Max and

how she is done *wifing*
and *kissing ass*."

Returning the Favor

"I don't know who I am when I look outside
or where the roads go," says Bobbi watching Ohio
Street from her windows, nothing familiar
or reliable, not memories,

not me, not simple acts like getting out of bed
or dressing; as a kid, I promised to build a mansion;
a wing for Bobbi and her husband, another
for my father and his wife; a third

for me. "Dad, look at the granite walls I made
for my mansion," my daughter says deploying tools
on the iPad screen playing Minecraft, a game
about living and going

on adventures, which reminds me of the promise
I made and how this life, unfortunately, leads nowhere
familiar, the end a tangle of panic and outbursts
you can't take back. "Go

fuck yourself, Buddy," Bobbi yells, then slams
the phone on its cradle because I can't visit every
day, or enough to fill the empty, lost spaces
collapsing on her.

Sweeter Than This

"Yes, I'd like coffee," says Bobbi
to Lily, the interim administrator who
slips between tables and fills empty

cups by the smile; the dining room
at Winterberry is full, rollators and quad
canes parked against the wall; a man

in a wheelchair a few tables away
stares at me. Bobbi asks for the caddy
of Sweet'n Low, then spills a wedge

of pink packets into her hand. "Want
any?" she asks. "No, thank you," I laugh.
"I'm not living longer than necessary."

Two Peas in a Pod

Mary has three lipsticks
on the table and uses crimson
to scribble on the backs

of monthly event calendars
she arranged into a slim booklet.
"I'm taking notes,"

she says in a voice barely
audible, the dining room filled
with a musician's

acoustic guitar; he's singing,
This Land Is Your Land. "Where's
my dress?" Mary says

suddenly alarmed, hands on
her ears, dementia's gross grip
squeezing off judgement

and reason. "You're okay,
Mary," I reassure her, patting my
shirt from across the table.

"You're wearing a raspberry
knit sweater with jeans. You look
gorgeous today."

"What are all these people
doing in my closet?" she replies
as lost as Bobbi who folds

and unfolds a stack of napkins
while grooving to the folk tempos
of Woodie Guthrie.

Choose Your Joy

"You have a birthday
next month," I tell Bobbi
and turn right on Union

street. "Not me, Mister,"
she replies. "Maybe you're
the one having another

birthday." "I'll be 50
in March," I pull into TD
Bank. "I'm wishing for

inner peace this year."
"Peace?" she scoffs, tooth-
less. "Forget that!"

Compassion

"I can't get them on my feet," Bobbi grumbles
when I ask about the shoes her sister sent, double
wide orthotics with Velcro closures. "Sit here,
Mom, so I can help." Undoing the zipper

front of her raggedy sneakers I ease them off
her feet as if they are nuclear bombs and the poodle
print socks slide off too. My mother's ankles are
thick, slabs of marbled meat. "Give me this

one first, Mom," I wiggle the piggy that went
to the market. Wipe lint off her heals. Apply lotion
even though touching her dry, cracked skin makes
me want to gag. "Press down," I instruct,

pulling her socks back up and screwing on her
new shoes, and I think about last offices, the custom
of laying out the body of a dead person—jewelry
removed, eyes closed, arms by their sides,

bladder drained, body washed and dressed in a
simple garment or shroud. Each shoe fits perfectly
when Bobbi toddles about the room to test them,
amazed like a child's first steps.

Emergency Care

Hunched at the kitchenette table
and pointing at Max who is sitting
in bed across the room, Bobbi

says, "Don't be mad, but I think
something's wrong with his throat.
I don't like to see my Maxie in

pain; I think we should take him
to the, the, damnit, you know." "Dog
doctor?" I fill in the words reclined

in the lounge chair by the window,
calendaring in my mind the last time
I changed his batteries. "I'll call

for an appointment with my vet."
"That would be nice," Bobbi lights
up like Barbara Stanwyck, film

star. "I feed him scraps, but can't
get him to swallow. It makes me sad
to see somebody so sweet and

gentle suffer like this. I love him so
much. I was going to take him myself.
I had the car keys in my hand, but I

wanted you to see him first so you
didn't think I was crazy or something
worse." "Are you ok, Max?" I ask

30

kneeling by the bed which triggers
jerky robotic gears which trigger his
head to turn towards me. "Bark,"

he replies, fleece tongue encrusted
with pieces of BBQ chicken tenders
and peachy, Chobani yogurt.

Dead People Calling

"Mom, what are you doing?"
I push into the studio
apartment and drop grocery bags
in the doorway;

Bobbi is sitting on the floor,
back against the kitchen
sink cabinet, hugging Max,
sobbing, glassy eyes;

Max is a mechanical therapy
dog, a soft robot, whose
heart beats when you pet her wavy
microchip sensitive fur;

"I don't know if my mother
or father can find me
here," Bobbi sobs. "It's nasty
and so windy outside."

Sliding down the opposite wall
I decide not to tell her Gram
and Pop are dead, [but then I realize,
she means their ghosts.]

Cahoots

Sam's arm is warm
when she puts it around
my neck. "If you help

gather your mother's
dirty underthings, I'll wash
and put them away."

Adult Diaper Rebellion

"What's the matter, Mom?" I say
alarmed at Bobbi's whimpering and
reluctance to talk. "I don't know

what happened," she sniffs. "Whatever it is we can fix it," I coo into the
phone. "I'm wet," she sobs, again,

elderly sobs of a child, "and my
bed's soaked too. Is it raining out?"
"Yes, Mom, like cats and dogs."

Sweet Mercy is Nobility's True Badge

When your mother says she wants to die,
and knowing Alzheimer's Disease destroys
brain tissue, not just neurons and synapses,

you Google states where doctors have
merciful authority to prescribe lethal doses
of medicine for terminally ill patients

who wish to end their suffering. Vermont
is closest. You could pick up Bobbi in Bangor
and be in Vermont in four hours and stay

at a hotel free using your rewards points.
This possibility brings hope for the first time
since you uprooted your mother from

Florida; maybe she does not have to suffer
the inevitable, total confusion, forgetting how
to eat and drink, dying of deficiency, but

the reverie ends once your Google search
lands on www.brainquality.org: *people with
dementia are not eligible for mercy yet.*

Filicide

"It's cold,"
Bobbi moans
while Rhonda
washes her

thighs with
a warm hand
towel. "Let's
get ready

for your son,"
she redirects
with a voice
melty as Milk

Duds. "Here's
fresh pants.
And let's fix
your hair."

"I don't have
a son," Bobbi
pushes Rhonda's
fingers aside.

Circle of Life

"Something is wrong
but I don't know what,"
says Bobbi folding,

unfolding, and folding
by unfolding her fleece
jacket again, "Here

you do it," she shoves
the fuzzy hood in my face.
I don't know what she's

doing either but act as
if I work at the Gap, fold
it neatly, then cram it in

the over-stuffed dresser
draw. "There it is," Bobbi
takes the garment back

out, again, shakes it open
like a picnic blanket, slips
a thin wrist into the

sleeve and pulls it inside
out, holding an arm above
her head; a white flag of

truce she huffs, "Would
you help me! I don't know
shit from more shit!"

37

Hardlined

Hands shaking Bobbi brings the landline
receiver to her ear; last week she threw away
the cordless phone, said it was broken

instead of returning it to its cradle for charging.
"Hello," she says to the dial tone. "Gary? Are you
there? Please pick up. I need you. I've got to get

out of here." Bobbi stands, now, eyes glazed,
and shuffles to the window, the phone stretching
from the wall jack like an umbilical cord.

Hearing Shadows

"Help!" Bobbi calls
out to Jim, her husband,
dead nearly two years.

All the lights are on,
2 AM. "Help, me, Jimmy,"
Bobbi calls out again,

but she's looking at me,
wide awake on the couch,
digging her grave.

Higher Power

"Ma, do you believe
in God?" asks her middle
son visiting from

California. Hugging
Max Bobbi replies, "I don't
know, honey; I never

think much about
those things." Scott nods,
then nervous laughs.

Bob Dylan Cover

Resident Assistant Jean
wheelchairs an old woman
into the common area

where it's standing room
only for Drake, the one man
show who plays guitar,

harmonica, and sings
once a month making rounds
at all the assisted living

facilities in northern Maine.
When Jean sets the wheelchair
brake and kisses the old

woman's cheek as easily
as kissing her own daughter's,
tears fill my eyes, Drake

singing, "The answer, my
friend, is blowin' in the wind.
The answer is blowin'

in the wind." "Yes, yes,
it is," says Bobbi, conducting
the band with her fingers.

Thanks for Nothing

"You don't do enough for me,"
says Bobbi, shaking, anxious from
an unreachable itch

on her back which I'm scratching
over a V-neck blouse. "Mom," I reply,
"I changed my entire life

to take care of you." "Well,"
it doesn't feel like it," Bobbi aims
her bug bite at my fingernails.

Imposter

Bobbi wants me to call her
son for help. "I *am* your son,"
my response reeks of

shock. "Your name might be
Gary, too," Bobbi replies, "but you
are not *my* son, Gary,

who knows what's what."
Bobbi's words buckle as if each
one is warped, twisted

out of shape. "When I see him,
Mom," I smile at my daughter sitting
nearby, (a sadlovefear smile

that my brain might forget her
one day, too,) "I'll give Gary your
message, have him call you."

Bobbie thanks me for knowing
what's what, says her son's voice
is a lot like mine.

43

Insight

"What do you think about?" I ask Bobbi,
who taptaptaps five Sweet'N Lows into a small
cup of Dunkin Donuts coffee. "What I do,"

Bobbi shakes her head and puzzles the empty,
pink packets inside a napkin, demented origami.
"What do you 'do?' " I pause, sipping

my Americano uncertain whether Bobbi is joking
or confused as algebra. "Nothing," she slaps me with
stormy eyes, then cranes her neck and smiles

at the young woman waiting for an iced latte.
"So you think about nothing?" I tease following
the arch of her logic, trying to sugar the

artificially sweetened mood. "Life is a bunch
of nothing!" Bobbi skewers the air with a stir stick
and my heart—terrified—tries to disagree.

It Doesn't Get Better

"I've never slept so much in my life,"
Bobbi slurs. "Do you think you can come
see me someday soon?" "Mom, we

spent the whole morning together,"
I groan. "I'll be back next week." "But
how will I get home? My clock says

9:35 PM. Monday. December. What is
this telling me?" "You had your hair styled
today," I redirect. "Elaine takes good

care of you and your hair. You can go
more often if you want." "Oh, that Elaine,
she does nice work, but a man at the

front desk said all the people here are
sleeping. How can that be? Nobody ever
told me, so what's next? What are we

doing now?" "Going to sleep, too, Mom.
We go to bed when it's dark out." "Not me,
Mister. I can't get home by myself, and

I don't know if I can sleep. I have tons
of paperwork that won't fix itself!" Bobbi
slams the phone, doesn't say goodnight.

Jabberwocky

"Let me tell you about your wife,"
Bobbi grumbles. "I mean, these people
around here bust my ass; they're not

nice; they look nice but screw you
over. My father was a good man; the men
here want to stick it to you; there's

never a good time or place for that.
I'm afraid I don't know about this other
key; I'm afraid in my own house."

Ken Kesey

"How's your mother?" Eileen shuffles over.
I am signing the visitor log at the reception desk.
"You *are* Bobbi's son, right?" "Yes," I reply,

"I'm the youngest." "I watched her slipping,
right out of the arms of two aides like a trust fall."
I glance at the open staircase. *Over ten steps*

to the first landing. Forty-five degree slope.
Bobbi must have bounced twice before striking
her head, I calculate. "I am so glad she's

alright," Eileen sighs. "This is some, *One Flew*
Over the Cuckoo's Nest, place. One minute you're
glad, then you're mad, and then you're glad

again. Like you have no vote. I guess we're all
walking in circles," Eileen seizes her quad-cane,
pats my hand, then shuffles off to Zumba.

47

Lost and Found

"I have a problem," says Bobbi,
white hair standing up. "What, Mom?"
I reply, hunting around the room

for her missing sneaker. "I can't stay
here," Bobbi sweeps sugar from the table
into her hand and dumps it back

on the table. "Why not, Mom?"
"I can't call my mother or father
and I have to talk with them,

but I don't know if they are alive."
"Gram's been dead over forty years,
Mom, and Pop nearly twenty,"

I reach behind the couch, pull out
a dusty sneaker like a baby being born.
"If you say so," Bobbi rolls her eyes.

Widespread Damage

"Nobody is at breakfast," Bobbi says into the TV
remote as though it's a walkie-talkie. "I don't know
what's wrong with this place," she shuffles

to the dresser, opens the bottom drawer, pushes stacks
of magazines aside and slips the remote into a tissue box
filled with peppermints. The electric wall heater roars,

blows dry, hot air into the apartment; Bobbi shivers,
whispers about being too hot, or too cold, and not being
able to reach the knob that adjusts the thermostat.

"How am I going to get out of here?" she says to Max.
"Max, Max, Jesus Christ! Where are you?" Bobbi panics,
then notices one end of Max's leash looped around her

wrist, the other end hooked to his collar, Max curled
at her feet. "There you are, my Maxie. I love you, Max."
Bobbi shuffles to the bed, pulls back the comforter,

a mountain printed on it. She lies down, head on a stack
of pillows. Max goes under the bed tethered by the leash.
Reaching for the nightstand Bobbi takes out a leather

purse from the bottom cubby. She squeezes it to her
chest, like a teddy bear, tears in her eyes; she mumbles,
sour gusts, but dementia does not translate.

Max

"Can you take me to get my dog?"
says Bobbi. "Mom, Max has a new home
with Judith and Dempsey."

"Well, I need him here. I miss my Max."
"I'm sorry, Mom. Max can't stay at Winterberry
anymore." "Why not?" "He wasn't getting

along with the other dogs." "Oh, no, really?
I didn't know that." "That's why I found Max
a brother to live with." "Ok, but I'm going

to bring him home anyway." "Mom,
Winterberry is home." "Well, I think I'm
going to bring him home anyway."

Humanitarian Aid

Kneeling at Bobbie's feet and trying to steady
her gory, papier-mâché fingers, I say, "I promise
not to hurt you, Mom. Your nails are too long

and sharp and catch on everything you touch."
Panicked Bobbi whimpers, shoulders pumping
like pistons. "Oh my God, what are you

doing!" she flinches and squeals when I clip
the middle fingernail which missiles into the kitchen.
I take a deep breath. I want to walk away, stop

caring and feeling responsible, let the state of
Maine deal with my mother's aging in place, but
that would be cruel; I don't want to be treated

cruelly if I live into my eighties. "When my
daughter was a baby," I say trying a new approach,
"her fingers were so tiny I was afraid I'd nip off

their tips, so I trimmed her nails with my teeth
instead of clippers. "Are you going to bite mine?"
asks Bobbi, horrified yet eager as a puppy.

Mercy Killing

"Shoot me in ten years if I am anything
like your mother," says Bev when I tell her
about Bobbi's barking robot golden-

doodle, a substitute dog for real Max
who has a new forever home with Judith
now. I explained how Bobbi insists

that I take robot Max to my vet because
mashed potato is stuck in his mouth. His
swallow, she told me, is broken. "I'll

take him while you're having lunch with
your friends," I suggested. "Then you won't
have to go out in the snow." "Nope,"

Bobbi fists the air. "Where he goes I go.
And there's another issue I want to discuss;
he's not shitting nearly enough either."

A Dunkin' Donut Worldview

"Look at my hands," Bobbi spits, jelly donut
in a wobbly tailspin. The shock on her face tracks
the sugar as it powders the table. "What the

hell!" she looks at me. "Are you a jelly donut
is half-empty or half-full kind of a lady?" "Half
dead," she sneers at her hands trembling

against her will. I wish I could time-travel back
before the diagnosis; I would hold Bobbi's hands
steady, edit the scenes in her life that amount to

Alzheimer's disease. "Your imbalance is eighty
years of caffeine, jelly donuts, and trouble, Mom."
"Why do you talk so foolish?" she points as if I

delivered an injustice greater than the lumps of
dementia proteins eating away her thoughts. "I'm
The Three Stooges, Mom," I reply, but she is

tottering for the emergency exit, now, her brain
on a collision course with every green leaf turning
brown, aware yet not aware of the seasons.

Tug of War

"I'm supposed to be your mother," Bobbi shifts
in her chair, rubs rose petals between her fingers,
"but I'm not mother material anymore. I'm

more like a little girl again, who needs her own
mother, but my mother has been dead for decades,
and you're . . . *Gary*—one of my sons, right?"

Anachronism

On the windowsill you are eighteen
months old. White winter boots. White mittens.
White Cossack hat, and a white wool duffel

coat contrasts with your mother's black,
faux fur. Posing for the picture Grandma is smiling.
Holding you. Rural Long Island. Nineteen

thirty nine when you lived in New Cassel,
metal wash basin upended against the woodshed.
Your narrow eyes look like my daughter's

eyes. Which surprises me. I never noticed
the likeness before so I pick up the plastic picture
frame for closer inspection. There is intensity

like the intensity that creases your face now
that you are eighty one, and "pleasantly demented."
Your doctor's diagnosis. Not mine. Without

thinking I pinch my fingers over your face to
zoom in—I laugh thinking how impossible it is for
Superman these days to find a telephone booth.

Pine Tree Inn

"Traveling or here for business?"
small talks the young man at the check-
in desk mousing the computer for a

room; lingering cigarette smoke
from the lobby entrance clings bitterly
to my jacket; I smell my father and

his wife chain-smoking Salem Lights
over forty years ago; "I'm here," I reply,
"because my pleasantly demented

mother fell down a flight of stairs,
right on her empty fucking head, so I
need a fucking place to sleep." The

young man squints; he is wearing a
Slayer t-shirt, The Unholy Alliance Tour,
2006, and like the still-point presence

of Lao Tzu he hands me a keycard
and says, "I hope it works out the way
it's supposed to work out, sir."

A Life is More Than Your Heart Beating

"It's a good thing we don't know what's in front of us,"
says Aunt Franny, Bobbi's sister-in-law, *88 years old and
still driving,* she emphasizes every time she calls

to check on Bobbi. "Your mother had such a good laugh,"
Aunt Franny reminisces. "Does she still laugh?" Yes, I reply,
then tell her about Mary and Mitchell, semi-independent

residents who live on the memory care side of Winterberry
Heights. Although Mary is technically married, Mitchell is her
dementia-husband who lives down the hall; one morning,

nuzzling each other's necks, holding hands, whispering
sweet nothings, and playing footsie under the bench, Bobbi
rumbled at their public display of affections. "They should

get a room!" I joked nudging Bobbi, and if she still wore
false teeth she would have spit-laughed them into the bushes.
"That's nice to hear," Aunt Franny chuckles. "She sure

could laugh and fuss, your mother; you're a good son for
all the time you spend with her." I tell Aunt Franny⟦I know
what Bobbi wants to say when she can't find her words.⟧

57

Facial Recognition

Sitting around after breakfast
Bobbi—glazed expression—nods
at me walking to their table,
resident assistants stacking plates
and glasses in brown bins

on rolly carts. "What now?"
says Bobbi, but it is not a question
as much as it is a concession.
"Let's go to your apartment," I suggest,
"check the fridge; or if you want,

we can go to Hannaford's."
Assembling the lid on a Styrofoam
cup crammed with eggs for robot
Max, Bobbi stands up, then steps aside,
not certain I'm her son

when I reach for her red sweater
draped behind the chair. "It's ok I go
with him, right?" Bobbi asks
Pat while looking over her shoulder
appraising me.

Rorschach Test

Pointing at chocolate splotches on her napkin
Bobbi squints. "I used to know this guy," she looks
at me as if she's reading the obituaries. "Not this

guy, though," Bobbi's finger taps another chocolate
splotch, lands like a question. "Can you tell me who's
running around with who these days?" "No, Mom,

but here's a fresh napkin," I take the splotched one,
fold it into squares. "Wait," she puts up a hand, "I'm
not finished with that yet." "Okay," I reply, "fair

enough, but let's go home and sort out your blouses;
the ones we bought today. Do you want them hung up
in the closet or stuffed in your draws?" "Yes, that's

how the mischief starts," Bobbi stands, seizes my
arm for balance. "I should put my face on first. Then
if another man sees me—well, let's not gossip."

Queen of Italian

We don't go to Dunkin' Donuts anymore,
so I bring coffees, light and sweet, to Bobbi,
now. "How's life?" I ask, biting into a

cinnamon raisin bagel, not toasted, cream
cheese oozing over my fingers. "Vaffanculo!"
Bobbi replies, powdered jelly donut in one

hand, glazed pumpkin Munchkin—orange
sprinkles—in the other, sunlight filling in the
seams around the drapes. Like a crown.

Save Our Ship

"I'm dying again," says Bobbi, buzzing like a hornet's nest,
and then she cries, "Oh, shit!" when the phone falls off the table.
"Please don't go anywhere, yet," her voice begs the empty
walls which will never bring comfort or look

familiar. "I need my papers." Bobbi doesn't mean to say
papers reaching for the phone hanging by its cord, whimpering
fear so real I feel it too, a current of static electricity. "Gary,
are you still there?" "Mom, turn the phone around,"

I call out, "you're talking into the wrong end." "I'm sorry,
what I've become. I didn't ever mean to be a bother to anybody,
especially you, but how soon can you get here because I can't
wait like you might think? I'm dying again."

Shame

"What can I do to help, Mom?"
I ask, Bobbi weeping into the phone,
and I can see her in my mind,

edgy, cast adrift at the kitchen
table, Sweet'N Low packets ripped
open, white crystals everywhere,

and the picture frame she keeps
dismantling, pieces piled up for me
to reassemble. "I can't do this

anymore," Bobbi sniffles. "I woke
up wet," she continues, unable to hold
back a whimper. "I feel so ugly."

Sisterhood of the Caring

"I'm Teresa Goodrich," she says
relaxing on a bench in the corridor
sipping apple juice. Teresa is

Bobbi's age, but there is a jewel
in her eyes that Bobbi doesn't have
anymore. "Look at you all spiffy

today," she lifts a Red Solo Cup
at Bobbi who replies with zigzags
of disordered syllables. "Your

mother was naked except for her
smile when she came out yesterday
for breakfast," says Teresa, "but

I got her situated. Isn't that right,
Bobbs?" Teresa makes another toast.
"Thank you," I reply, a ping of

sadness rippling through me. I want
to comment about the fellowship here,
old ladies helping old ladies, but

like Bobbi, I can't find the right
words or maybe words don't matter
as much as helping each other.

Small Civil Matters

Amber sets a bowl of steaming,
microwave oatmeal, pitcher of warm
milk, and packets of brown sugar

on Bobbi's paper placemat. "No,
I can't chew those anymore," Bobbi
waves away the plastic ramekin of

plump raisins; then she dumps all
the fixings together, adding globs of
butter. "This is my new favorite,"

she shovels three, drippy forkfuls
into her mouth—and shakes with joy.
"Use the spoon, Mom," I hold mine

up for comparison. "It's gross and
indecent to fork the oatmeal," I laugh
kicking Bobbi's leg under the table.

Broken Beyond Repair, cha-cha-cha

The landline phone rings again; the bathroom
fan rattles like it's choking; Bobbi's purple pants
sag from the showerhead; a nightclub of silk
blouses lineup on hangers

across the towel rack; hot water sprays from
the sink's faucet; blue, tinted toothpaste ooze spits
out of its tube; stinking Depends overflow the
trash container. "Maxie," Bobbi cries

for help, sprawled on the floor, left eye bruising
up already from the fall, smacking her head on tile.
"Maxie, I almost died," she cries out again,
examining the medical alert system

looped around her neck; she has no idea what
the red button does anymore; no idea that a nurse
will be in her room in less than three minutes
if pressing the button made sense

to her or if she still knew that the ringing in the
other room is the telephone and that I'm on the other
end and could call the reception desk for help,
but like she said yesterday when

we were sitting in the common area watching
the other residents merengue from folding chairs
with Trish, the Zumba lady who comes once
a week, "Nothing works anymore."

Striking Gold

I pass groceries to Bobbi
from the counter, and she shuttles
each item into the refrigerator:

cases of Boost on the bottom
shelf; mandarin oranges in juice
on the door; Kraft singles go

in the cheese bin; a dozen hard
boiled eggs are assembled in a bowl,
then covered with napkins.

"Mom, I have a surprise for you,"
I tell her once she's done fussing, done
rearranging SpaghettiOs.

Digging into my front pocket
I can't wait for Bobbi's red carpet,
Barbara Stanwyck smile.

"Cup your hands," I say and drop
her bracelet-watch into them. "I had
a jeweler replace the battery."

"That's not my watch," Bobbi
spits. "What did you do with my good
watch? All my things disappear!"

"Mom, that is your watch. Read
the inscription." Fitting the Timex
over her wrist she examines it

as if she's appraising the heavens
for truth and says, disgusted, crushed,
and old, "I'll make do, I guess."

Lean Into Each Day With Grace

Ten Splendas later Bobbi says,
"I'm not dead yet," then sips a café
con leche steaming with caramel

drizzle. "When I saw you hunched
over in the dining room, I thought you
were dead." "I'm not ready for that,"

she laughs and points, eyes shifting
from her jelly donut to fearsome tears:
"Are my parents still alive?" "No,

Mom," I shake my head biting into
a Bangor blues breakfast bagel. Eggs,
sausage, and a schmear of sadness.

Telephone Game

"Hello?" Bobbi swats the telephone
cord as if it were a coiled up snake, pushes
the cradle across the table, then finally
picks up. "Mom, your phone isn't

broke, after all," I say into my cellphone
sipping coffee, sitting right across from her
in the apartment. "Gary? Is that you?
I'm so glad you finally

called." I reach for my mother's hand.
Tell her she can hang up now, but her face
twists, her mouth angry. "Shush," she
bites. "I'm talking with my son."

Tessie's Ghost

Bobbi gazes into a plate of vegetable
tetrazzini. "Where did she go?" she jumps.
"Who, Mom?" I reply, confused. "I was

asking her a question," Bobbi points
at the half-empty glass of juice. "Now she's
gone." "The waitress?" I bite the inside

of my cheek. "My mother," Bobbi replies
as if Tessie has *not* been dead for over forty
plus years. "Did she say anything?" "I

don't remember," Bobbi looks around the
dining room for Grandma, convinced she was
right here. "What did you ask her?" I sound

matter-of-factly. "If there's a God, does
he know what's happening to me?" Bobbi
swirls the creamy pastas on her fork.

Tracheotomy

Snoozing, nuzzling Max, Bobbi's eyes flutter
and struggle behind baggy lids, as if she's dreaming
an action movie. "She sleeps a lot," says Kayla,

a tattooed med-tech, who taps Bobbi on the arm.
"Time for meds, hon," she chirps and Bobbi opens
her mouth like a chickadee so Kayla can spoon

the crushed pills mixed with strawberry pudding.
Bobbi swallows, makes a yuck face, then looks at me.
"Good," she says. "You're here. We really need

to talk. I want help with my dog; he is not eating,
again." She sticks a fingernail in his mouth and dried
whoknowswhat catapults. "I want you to cut him,

here, so I can get food in his belly," she spreads
crusty fur on his neck. I offer to take Max to my vet,
but she says there is a knife in her back I can use.

Voicemail

"Hello, hello, Gary? It's Mom.
It's Thursday, 12:22 in the morning.
You said you were coming to get
me on Thursday. I don't know

what you're thinking, but I can't
do anything. I don't know where the
hell I am. I'm here, in room," she
stammers, can't say 201, yet

perseveres: "I'm here where I sleep,
now. It's raining, I think. Call me, so
I can talk right. And be careful
driving in the rain, ok?"

Until Dementia Do Us Part

Bobbi and Jim married, a justice of the peace
service, the summer before I went into middle school,
my daughter's age; for the first time in 38 years
Bobbi's fingers are slim; her knuckles

rawboned and not fleshy enough anymore to
keep jewelry from slipping off, from being wrapped
in tissue with everything else she wraps in tissue;
searching the pockets of her pants

hangered in the closet, my heart is heavy: "Mom,
your diamond ring, you're not wearing your wedding
ring." Bobbi swigs warm Pepsi, then sucker
punches, "Marriage is temporary!"

WElls-1-5279

"Before you go," Bobbi sounds agitated,
"can you tell me my mother's phone number?"
"Mom, I'm sorry, Gram died years ago,

when I was a boy." "What! Nobody told
me!" Then Bobbi wails into the phone. "I'm
so sorry, Mom." "It's not your fault," she

moans, "but before you go, I have paper
and a pencil now. What's my mother's phone
number, again? I need to talk to her."

Money or Your Life?

"Are you applying that fancy
lotion Dr. Singer prescribed?" I ask
butter-knifing into a fatty piece

of pork chop, soaking it in apple
cinnamony glops and eyeing the dry
blotchy red spots on Bobbi's

arms. In between spitting bits of
garlic, smashed potato into a napkin,
she snorts, "I'm too busy for that

bull's shit." Then she throws up
her hands as if I were aiming a gun
chest level, stick'em-up style.

Please Leave a Message

Bobbi doesn't hear the phone
until the third ring. By the sixth
a digital voice says, *Please*

leave a message. "Hey, Mom.
Are you there? Just calling to say,
Hello. So hi! You said stay on

the phone if the answering
machine picks up first. I know
you need time to get to the

phone from your chair. How's
that bad hip today? I'll sing while
I wait, 'Strangers in my head

exchanging glances / I wonder
where she is / I guess she's a cat
napping.'" Then Bobbi picks

up the phone. "Shit! Shit! Shit!"
she bangs the receiver on the wall,
shipwrecked like a tombstone.

Adrift in The Bliss of No More Knowing

Standing by the telephone ringing Bobbi organizes junk
mail into stacks of financial records she'll work on later and
wraps the curlicue cord around her bent, arthritic fingers,

a one-handed Cat's Cradle; then a door slams—Brad, a
med-tech, helping Dorothy manage with her walker. "Doesn't
that tick you off," Bobbi says to herself about their muffled

voices and picks up the telephone, studies the LCD display,
the smooth, plastic body and pushbutton lights. "Mom, speak
into the mouth-piece end, the cord end." "Hello," Bobbi

replies after a pause, her best secretarial voice. "Can I help
you?" "Mom, it's me," but my name doesn't register. "I heard
ringing but didn't know what the heck to do," she admits,

then plants the handset on the table as if our brief convo
happened in her head; shrugging she plucks yellowed strands
from her robe and believes she's dressed in linty sunlight.

Paper Tail With a Push Pin

"I want to listen to your heart and lungs,"
says Dr. Carroll pulling a stethoscope out

of her L.L.Bean boat-tote. Bobbi's eyes
shift around the room. "I see that everyday

but don't know what it is?" Bobbi points
vaguely. "What?" replies Dr. Carroll. "Over

there." Bobbi points again in the vicinity
of the kitchen." Dr. Carroll asks if she

is referring to the VA flag on display over
the refrigerator. "No, no," Bobbi is annoyed

and toddles into the kitchen area. "This
is where I keep my diet Pepsi," Bobbi opens

the refrigerator door, closes it, "but what's
this?" she grabs the handle right above. "That's

the freezer," Dr. Carroll answers approaching
Bobbi with the stethoscope as if she is

playing pin the tail on the donkey. "I want
to listen to your heart and lungs," she

says again. "Oh dear," Bobbi replies. "I
don't think I have them right now." "Well,"

Dr. Carroll reaches with the resonator, "let
us get a good listen and find out."

Gesundheit

A fleet of zero-turn mowers zip around
as three guys with gas blowers push leafy
debris at their Black Bear Lawn Care

truck parked outside Bobbi's windows
which are open wide to clear the retching
piss smell. "It's so loud," she cringes,

then sneezes, scooping up a tissue, but
it's not a tissue, it's a sock with a cartoon
hunter knitted into it, who is carrying

a cartoon rifle that shoots a *Just Kidding*
cartoon flag; Bobbi swivels her hand inside
as if it makes sense, puppets the sock with

wiggly fingers, snatches her nose, blows,
then honks and honks until a skein of geese
migrate across the room in V-Formation.

Monkey Chases the Weasel

"How's your mother?" Bobbi asks, then kisses
her unstuffed dog as if it were a baby cooing. "My
daughter's basketball team made the playoffs,"

I steer the conversation away from the awkward
sinkhole, show her pictures on my cellphone. "You
never said anything about a daughter?" she fake

smiles. "Here, Mom," I open a 12-piece box of
Munchkins, redirect with a wonderland of chocolate
glaze and another picture of Meri chest passing

the ball to Taylor which reminds me of the wood
block I found hidden in one of Bobbi's dresser draws,
stamped with the word, BELIEVE, in red, cursive

letters. *Believe in what?* I said to the empty room:
God? Bigfoot? Basketball? "Taste one, the glaze is
made with extra love." Bobbi reaches in the box,

scratches around like a chicken in a coop. "Pinch,
pinch," I show off using my finger and thumb, popping
one in my month; then she pinches one, too, then

another, and then she dumps the box of crumbs on
the table. "How's your mother?" she asks, then kisses
her unstuffed dog, making no sense of this mess.

Daily Bread

"Tuesday,
Mom, in two days."
"It's Sunday?

Really? Ok.
Tuesday, I guess,"
Bobbi replies,

shaky, on the edge
of confused tears. "All
I need is you to

tell me you love
me." "I do, Mom,
I love you."

Karma

I stopped at Bobbi's
to give her a kiss
because in each of us
is all of us.

Assisted Living

Orange sunset lights the horizon
ferrying home on yesterday's last boat;

Blue Hill mountains are exposed by negative space;
Rick, the engineer, updates about the Pats

vs Jaguars, 14 to 7, second quarter; Lily trolls
Facebook on her smartphone; Lee jokes,

thanks me for choosing Maine Department
of Transportation as my preferred mode of travel;

my daughter, who loves sports, is reading,
Point Guard, a novel about basketball.

I shut my eyes, hear my mother sobbing
into the phone, "Please, help me find home."

Alzheimer Elegy

My neighbor suggests that I
might be in mourning over Bobbi
even though she is alive, assisted

living in Bangor by the airport.
We expect, at some point or another,
to make funeral arrangements for

our parents, pick out the caskets,
order flowers, bury them, move on
with our own lives, yet how do

you move on when your mother calls
in the middle of the night cursing, *Fuck
needlepoint!* Closure, my brother

reassures me. Your mother needs
closure. (Before she can be finished
with this living but not living.)

II: MEMORY CARE

No Cure Unit

Dear Memory
Care Visitor, Please
remember to

secure the door
behind you and leave
with no followers.

Center Point

Bobbi toddles from the bed
to the closet to the bathroom to
the end table to the dresser

to the bed again, red-eyed
from sobbing. "Mom, please,"
I kiss her head, coaxing

the dead to stop living, "you
have my consent. If you need
it." Then she hugs me even

tighter, saying nothing, and
she rubs my back, small circles,
no endings, no beginnings.

Golden Age of Whatever's Left

On the flat-screen tv in the sitting room Dinah
Shore sings, "Crying on the Inside," then Paul Anka
teen idols *The Ed Sullivan Show*, then song clips

of Patti Page and Kay Starr flash black and white,
and I ask Bobbi, "Was that your music growing up?"
"No," she snaps, shoulders swinging, dirty socks

tapping. Where am I exactly?" she leans close to
my face. "Heaven, Mom," I take her hands and we mash
potato to Frankie Laine, then The McGuire Sisters.

Doppelgänger

Kyna skates to our table, digital camera dangling
on a lanyard from her wrist. "Want me to take your
picture?" Bobbi says no, but I reply, "Absolutely,"

and drag my chair closer, pressing my face to Bobbi's,
wrapping an arm around her neck. "Say, *memory care*,"
I joke before Kyna asks us to say, *cheese*, and Bobbi

is already reaching to see herself in the demented world
of Alzheimer's disease. "Darling, you look *mah-vel-ous*,"
I wisecrack in my best Billy Crystal, Fernando

accent and Bobbi replies pointing at the man sitting
beside her in the pic, face pressed to hers, arm draped
around her neck, "That's your son, isn't it?"

Art of Mindfulness

Bobbi Swan Lakes in her chair,
opera on the radio, a woman's graphic
voice, Russian and vivid. "Your

baby is beautiful," I say to Bobbi
kissing the doll's head. "Is she your
baby?" "No," Bobbi sighs, turns

the baby in her lap to face her.
"Look at his eyes. They are so blue,"
she admires. "What's your baby's

name?" I ask. "Scott," she replies
which I didn't expect because Scott is
my older brother. "He's Nancy's

baby," she nods. My father's second
wife was Nancy. You have to let go here
of all you know, all you don't know.

Lady Luck

Walking in the opposite direction and
shlepping a burden of bulky laundry bags
over her shoulders, a resident assistant

I have never seen before sings, "Somebody is having her lucky day." Bobbi's arm
is hooked into mine; I am balancing a tray

from Dunkin' Donuts. It amazes me how
people here are not drained of all their extra
love and goodness after grinding ten hour

shifts, how they don't go home gutted,
nothing left to give their own families. *Luck
is,* I want to reply, *being alive, not a few*

jelly donuts and coffees, but that would
be heartless. I choke it down and wish Trish
(I read her nametag) a lovely Tuesday.

Family is Family

"HELP. HELP ME. PLEASE HELP ME ALREADY,"
shakes Memory Care like an air-raid siren, and nine women
at various stages of dementia and dying look up alarmed

from their midmorning snacks of gooey bread pudding; Diane
wants to know if somebody is hurt; Pat nervous-giggles; Caroline
shakes her head, continues to dress her dolls, and the med-tech,

sorting pills at her mobile drug station, says a new *customer*
cries day and night since her sister dropped her off. "Your father
came to see me," Bobbi interrupts. "How was that visit, Mom?"

I reply, curious as light since my father left us when I was
two. "Happy comes but not with your father," Bobbi shrugs,
then spits another sad, polished raisin in a paper towel.

Rotation of the Earth

Befuddled Bobbi pulls at bulky clothes. "I've got this thing,"
she wiggles like a toddler who has to go potty. "What, Mom?
What do you need?" I throw my hands in the air and she

responds by reaching behind and inside her adult diaper. "I'm
so fucking itchy," she cries. "There are tasks," I grimace but smile,
"a mother has to do for herself." Bobbi stops wiggling and gazes

at me as if I am the master key to every mystery. "Mom, you
have to scratch your own ass," I shrug. "It's meant to be, basic
law of the universe, *sons don't scratch their mothers' asses.*"

Incontinence

Wearing light-blue adult diapers
Hospice provides Bobbi sits on the toilet,
trying to pee. "If I stand

up," she shouts, "I'm all wet
again. I don't know what's going on
with me anymore." *I could leave*

right now, I think, standing by
the door, getting air, *and she'd never know,*
but I would know.

Where's the Baby, There's the Baby

A stripped down, lonesome version on the radio of Johnny
Cash plucking a guitar, he growls, "I keep my eyes wide open
all the time," and then Dimpy tells anybody who will listen
she has to go to the toilet, so I point out the bathroom

again; Rose fills a glass of cranberry juice with leftover
brussels sprouts from lunch that look like testicles floating
in a laboratory beaker; Denise, passing by, taps my arm,
sits across the room and spoons crushed pills mixed

with grape jelly in Cora's mouth; she winces as if tasting
a wedge of lemon for the first time; Bobbi is looking down,
now, hands resting on the table, *Animals, Animals, Silly
Animals,* upended, splitting its binding, loose pages

dogeared; it's as though Bobbi is pondering, trying at once
to conjure the past, predict the future, and escape the dreariest
moments of her present confusion; she looks at me—a time
lapse video—80 years compressed into seconds. "Gary!"

she says, jolts of lightning in her voice, head jerking up,
surprise and relief in her brown, starless eyes, startled that I am
still sitting right beside her sipping coffee. "Peekaboo, Mom,"
I joke for my benefit, then plant a kiss on her head.

Land of the Free and Brave

Bobbi drags the other chair closer, then picks the
dried crud off the seat; she doesn't know what it is
when I ask, so I soak and wring a wad of paper

towels and apply them to the brown, chipped mess
which like a practical joke transforms the room into
a toilet; gagging I wipe shit off the chair and think

about Jess, a Facebook meme she posted about
dementia, how the demented still have eyes to see,
ears to hear, how the afflicted are still individuals

and not to let go of them because they are still the
same people; but this Bobbi is not my mother, not the
fussy woman who slipcovered furniture with plastic;

no logic or bold belief will convince me that Bobbi
has any well-being left; if she could still add two and
two together, she would never shit herself again

or live with Alzheimer's, not for one second, not
if dying with dignity laws included individuals with
final memory loss as terminal as stage-four cancer.

The Third Mind

"I don't like the word,
Jim, when you say

we were married," spits
Bobbi hugging a new

teddy bear she insists
is a sneaker. "No, that's

wrong," she frowns, then
Etch A Sketches her

head as if she can shake
her thoughts clear.

Nothing But Love

Rubbing Verdi's shoulders,
gentle back and forth strokes,
she rests her head on John's

arm; I am sitting across the
room with Bobbi, who picks
at the knotted drawstring

on her pants; Verdi's wheelchair, locked in place, has pockets
like a motorcycle has leather

saddlebags. "Mom, stop with
that knot. Let's eat lunch before
the pasta sauce gets cold."

"Then help me," Bobbi grinds,
starts to stand. "I'll take my pants
off but I don't want you to get

excited." I forget my mother
thinks I want to fuck her, that
I'm one of her husbands.

"Sit, Mom. We'll take care of
that later," I ease her back into
the chair, fighting grief, and

John, the only male med-tech
on staff in Memory Care, packs
Verdi's wheelchair pockets

with towels for wiping drool,
a spill-proof water bottle, and a
yellow banana peel sack

of Bananagrams, a word game
Verdi hasn't played in years, but
the lettered tiles are a comfort.

Raspberry

Jelly donut dripping off her
lips Bobbi looks at me
as if I'm pretty as a picture and
says, "You are really

handsome." "I get my looks
from my mother," I reply
nibbling a pumpkin munchkin,
then ask: "You know her,

right?" Probing my face for a
toehold, eyes unable to find
a grip, she shakes her head, "No,
I don't think so."

Child Care Center

"These two were playing
tug-of-war with Shirley's cane,"

says Kyna, pointing at Bobbi
who called her a bitch

when she separated them
during a squabble at yesterday's

snack time. "Now that's the
mother I remember growing up

around," I reply nodding my
head. "It's alright, though," Kyna

defends them both, "we all
have bad days once in a while."

Snag

I clip
Bobbi's
gory

hangnails;
her hands are
soft

as tissue.
"I get them
caught

on my
clothes,"
she

bites
her dry
lips

flinches,
fingertips
raw,

afraid
I will cut
them.

"Trust
me, Mom,
I am

never
going to
make

this any
worse than
it is."

Avenue of No Escape

Earthquaking hands and out of breath, as if she has run
a 5K around Memory Care, Bobbi flips pages in the picture
book, *We're Going To The Zoo*, then points at the wall,

at the red tiled roof villa tucked in a valley of tranquil,
rolling hills and patchwork emerald pastures, where vineyard
vine brushstrokes mix with the sky, autumn colors like

bonfires. "Makes you want to step inside and walk away
from reality, doesn't it?" I regard the Monetesque print, large
as a flat-screen tv. "What a pretty dog," Bobbi replies, irons

the wrinkled pages of the picture book where a sea otter
pup is washed up on the beach, cute and wide-eyed. "She sure
is," I say as Lynsey from housekeeping sidles up to us. "Did

anyone call you? Your mother had an accident. Not a go
to the hospital accident. She pooped on the floor, tracked it
all over the place before anybody realized. We used rug

cleaner on the mattress too, but some of her magazines and
family pictures, and the pieces of art that your daughter made
were too gross to save." "Thanks a billion, Lynsey—for

not trying to save them," I reply, ignoring the muffled cries
for help from an apartment down the hall. "Help me, please,"
a desperate voice moans. I look at Bobbi, I look at the red

tiled roof villa tucked in a valley of rolling hills. "Let's get
the fuck out of here," I point at the bonfire skies, the emerald
pastures, and her hands quake, 7.3 on the Richter scale.

No End to Caring

As if we are old
high school buddies,
the homeless guy

says, "I don't think
I could be happier than
never," when I roll

down my window.
Please Kelp a Veteran
is printed on a piece

of cardboard. I've
been giving him money
for months, ever

since Hospice started
giving Depends and Boost
to Bobbi, and extra

baths and packages
of her favorite red striped
peppermints. "God

bless, sir," he salutes
and I hand him another
two dollars for kelp.

May the Wind be Always at Your Back

Here's to living good," I toast my travel coffee
mug to Bobbi's mug of hot chocolate. "I don't think
I could eat it," she replies calm now but no less

confused after a "physical altercation" the report
read. "She hit another resident," the med-tech said
telling me their story, "and then it was full on

MMA." Kyna refereed. "Is that good?" Hadley
interrupts us, sittings across the table, wiping chicken
stir-fry puree from her mouth. Hadley is new

to Memory Care; you can tell because she hasn't
lost her wedding ring yet. "What's the matter with
you!" Bobbi bawls, flings her hands in the air,

nostrils flaring, as if she's the crime boss Russell
Bufalino, Joe Pesci's character in *The Irishman*, face
bristling, that ruined intensity that doesn't let up.

Complicated Grief Therapy

"Don't let your mother's emotions
stop you from visiting or spending time

with her; if it's sunny, take a walk; if
it's raining, watch a video; there's, *I Dream*

of Jeannie or *Bewitched* on the shelf;
she loves those shows; maybe she'll cry

less if you distract her," Alisa suggests
when I sign out at the front desk. But when

I turn on the radio in my truck, Lemmy
from Motorhead whales out equally sensible

insight, *Don't believe in miracles don't
even try I know the law I know how to die.*

Weeping Garden

"Do you want me to go
home?" I say, moving aside
the succulent plant I gave

her last week, orange spice
flowers that suggest October.
"I don't have to stay long

if it's going to upset you
today." Bobbi sits across the
table, grief draining from

her eyes like blood from a
puncture wound. "My parents
are in Los Angeles," she

chokes, mixing up people,
places, and things in her head,
a game of Boggle of nobody

gets out alive. "Mom," I kiss
her cheek, "Do you think about
dying?" "Yes," she weeps,

brown, deadheaded petals
in her hand, "but I'm scared
of flying. All by myself."

Head Start Program for Seniors

"Whose coat is this?" Lynette says
about the brown winter coat with faux fur
trim around the hood that is balled up
on the table in the common-room

where I'm trying to get Bobbi to sit
for lunch: pork chops, apple chutney, green
beans, and biscuit; Lynette picks up the
brown winter coat with faux fur trim,

admires the softness on her face, slips
it on, then slinks away like an episode of
Kleptomaniac. "That's mine," Bobbi
reaches out, the look on her face

desperate as a four-year-old on guard
at her toybox. "My father bought that for me
when I was a girl," Bobbi pinches flaky
flesh from a warm, buttery biscuit.

Swimming Hole

"My life is blowing away," says Bobbi, mug of
hot chocolate shaking in her hands. "Good for the soul,
right?" I reply sidestepping her comment, focusing
instead on relishing the last few

cocoa-peppermint swallows. "Absolutely, Mister,"
she nods, takes another sip, then looks at Pat, a memory
care neighbor, sitting with us in the common area;
Pat is dozing, eyes heavy as maple

syrup. "This is my husband," Bobbi says to Pat
anyway. "We're married," she demands. "I call him my
son, but we're married." "It doesn't matter, Mom,"
I reassure her, but in my head I say, *It*

doesn't matter but it matters. "This is Pat, my good
friend." Bobbi offers her mug to Pat, but she's still dozing;
Bobbi had a friend named Pat McLean who remarried
when I was a kid and became Pat

McClaw; wondering if she thinks this is the same
Pat from Long Island, I ask, but Bobbi says she never lived
anywhere else except here and doesn't know any other
Pats. "She's not home if you ever look

in the back rooms." Bobbi's thoughts derail. "Who?"
I ask. "My mother!" "Gram comes to visit?" I say, hiding
my surprise since Gram died when I was in eighth or
ninth grade. "What the hell am I talking

about!" Bobbi sighs, sips the last bit of whip cream,

overturns her mug, dribs of chocolate spill, and we watch
the confluence of sweet rivulets meander downstream
and pool at the edge of the table.

Vaffanculo

A lukewarm washcloth I scour crust
from Bobbi's eyes. She tries to resist,

move her head, but can't. "Have you used
your sparkle word this week?" "Fuck

off!" Bobbi replies in translation, sparkles
flying. I laugh so loud she shushes me.

Rocky Horror Picture Show

Slumped in a chair at a table in the dining room
Bobbi nods in and out of consciousness from the
higher dose of OxyContin, *The Golden Girls*

on the tv booming from the common area: Sophia
suggests to Blanche that her breasts are not what they
used to be and the studio-audience laughter makes

me wince like it's 1981, again. My brother lives
in a filthy apartment with his girlfriend, pregnant with
my niece. I am twelve. The elevator smells rotted,

Bobbi remarks. Jerry answers the door; we follow
him into the kitchen where Kathy, addicted to heroin
and methadone maintenance, is slumped in a chair

by the window, lit cigarette dangling, smoke knitted
into a veil that wraps around her neck; Jerry acts as if
nothing is wrong, pours a cup of coffee, adds red

liquid from their stash, Kathy nodding in and out
of consciousness. "I have to go, Mom," I kiss Bobbi
on her sweaty forehead. "I'll see you tomorrow."

Gratitude

"Thanks for everything," I say
to Bobbi adjusting a pillow under
her backside and she looks

at me as if I'm a stranger. Alicia,
the med-tech, suggests that moving
her every two hours prevents

bedsores. "Yeah, like what?"
Bobbi replies, her voice a crevice
of scorpions, claws snapping.

Dignity

"I'm here to help,"
says Berg showing Bobbi
a clean adult diaper

in his hand. "Hold
my shoulder, I got you,"
his voice reassures.

First Frost

I swirl peanut butter into a steaming bowl
of oatmeal and think about Bobbi toddling in
circles asking what the goddamn noise—

the phone ringing off the hook—is all about,
and then, desperate, I am holding a pillow over
her face until she doesn't mix smithereens

of donut with cheesy macaroni or the corned
beef. My brother reassures me there will be no
autopsy, old ladies dying in their sleep, shit

happens every day, your mother, she's ready
and doesn't want to live like this; I'm ready too,
I reply but don't want to spend the rest of my

life in prison for anybody. No autopsy, little
brother; then he cites The Three Stooges, *Take
your time, but hurry up. Nyuk, nyuk, nyuk.*

Law of Conservation of Bobbi

Denise, a med-tech who will quit
next Wednesday because Memory Care
is a revolving door of turnovers and

hardships, plungers a dose of liquid
Ativan into Bobbi's mouth, lips shaking,
hands shaking, shoulders shaking

as if gale force winds rush alongside
the rushing of blood in her veins, 41knots
of flesh, bones, and primal confusion

in her brown, twitchy eyes. "Do you
have pain?" I put my hand over Bobbi's
thin, arthritic hand. "I want out," she

mutters, and I imagine her diaphanous
soul separating from her decrepit material
form, rising to the florescent lights

and sailing across the common room,
through the walls, into the trees where it
continues to rise and expand, wispy

fragmented energy transferring into the
warm, yellow, March sun patrolling over
the frozen Penobscot River in Bangor.

Full Mouth Extraction

Bobbi's false teeth say, "Do you remember
the husband and wife who lived together when
I had my place on the assisted living side of

Winterberry? They were younger, in their late
sixties, but he had advanced-stage Parkinson's or
multiple sclerosis or some other frightening

condition that confined him to a wheelchair;
he could hardly move, his face frozen in a shriek
of anxiety like *The Scream*, that iconic painting

by Edvard Munch; my memory was gone by
then; I was afraid to admit it and I was angry too,
shitting my Depends but there was nothing I

could do; I know we only have the time we're
given, I don't expect to live forever, but my worst
nightmare is coming true; Nell, his wife, spoon-

fed all his meals, *The Scream* in the wheelchair;
she dressed him; she wiped his ass! My father was
helpless at the end too, and I said put a pillow

over my head if I am ever totally helpless; I was
joking but as serious as shitting myself; there is a
meme one of the hospice nurses keeps reading

to me from Facebook about dementia; she's a
lovely girl who hums when she brushes my hair;
"Dementia," it says, "My eyes do see, My ears

do hear, I am Still Me, so let's be clear, My
memory may fade, My walk may slow, I am ME
inside, don't let Me go." What a stinking load

of horseshit! I stopped being me, stopped being
Bobbi, stopped being useful when my son locked
me in these haunted-rooms of Memory Care."

All We Want is Love

"You bring me light," says Bobbi
as I guide a forkful of shredded egg
sandwich to her lips; there is

a familiar focus in her eyes and a
clarity to her words, but neither lasts
more than a wink; I do not want to

watch my mother dying today, but
we do not get to cherry pick when life
needs or does not need us most.

Senior Citizen Discount

"Where's Momma?" Loretta brightens
when it's my turn at the register. "She can't
travel like she used to," I reply pinching
a few bills out of my wallet.

"I haven't seen you guys in a while and
was wondering." "Hospice checks-in now
practically daily." Loretta's eyes shift at
the mention of Hospice;

her husband died recently. "I'm sorry,"
she says. "I really enjoyed talking with Momma.
I'm going to miss her." Then she hands me
a bag with our donuts and fits

two coffees steaming into a coffee tray.
"I sure hope you didn't mind me calling her
Momma." "It was sweet, Loretta. Bobbi
loved talking to you, too," I nod

waiting for a final tally. "Well, *OK* then.
You take care," Loretta says, avoiding my eyes
because she knows I expect her to tell me
how much, but the tears

she's holding back say something else.
Pointing Loretta signals at the person in line
behind me and asks, "What will it be
this morning, hon?"

Happy Ending

Loraine from Hospice places a hand
on her shoulder, and Bobbi is startled
awake in her chair, as if she can't

believe she's still alive. Lunch hour
is over and residents mull around the
tables. "Hey, Honey, do you want

me to take you *home*? I can help with
tasks." Bobbi doesn't answer as much as
she consents, mixed mumbled words

spilling out of her like a lottery of
random people, places, and time. "Two,
four, four," Bobbi looks at Loraine

now and points at the room-number
plate beside her door. "I guess. I don't
know. We can try," says Bobbi

wobbling like a loaded spring and
knocks lightly. "No, we just push right
in," Loraine instructs, opens the door,

then leads her inside like a dancer;
after fussing in the closet as if it were
the kitchen, filling cups with water,

stacking them to dry, Bobbi is tired
and let's Loraine guide her to the couch
where she scoops up filthy not-Max,

and she doesn't have the energy to
object when Loraine removes her black,
clunky shoes. "Do your feet hurt,

hon," Loraine's voice is cherry, the
lollipop you pick when you're a kid at
the doctor's office. Bobbi doesn't

reply. Loraine squeezes lotion in her
hands, rubs Bobbi's stiff, rawhide feet;
on the tv is a commercial about how

nothing satisfies more than Snickers
ice cream; Bobbi's eyes are heavy; they
flutter, they shut, then she falls asleep.

Direct Cremation

Nurse Rex called
to tell me she ordered

a hospital bed for
Bobbi's room. "Expect

decline," she said,
"the next few weeks."

Life Alert

Balancing a tray of coffee, hot chocolate, Munchkins,
and my laptop I thumb the four-digit code into the keypad
that unlocks Memory Care; the door clicks, a light turns
green, and Bobbi is sleeping sitting up in the common area,
other women at various stages of dementia

and sickness sitting there too, Carol picking at scrambled
eggs and honeydew melon, Diane trying not to be seen covers
her face with a napkin, Frances cradling a naked baby doll;
the med-tech Denise whose Army son recently graduated boot
camp smiles, says hello cheery as a bowl of candy

red apples and tells me how my mother dressed herself
this morning. Like she is learning instead of dying. "Mom,"
I kiss her head and whisper, "are you done with this life
yet?" Bobbi's eyes open slowly, spot the box of Munchkins,
and she replies, "No, I'm trying to keep it."

In the Garden

Beacon Hospice chaplain asks Bobbi
if she wants to sing with Elvis; Bobbi nods,
then waits while Gail warms up the

iPad; once music fills the dying room,
Bobbi is in kindergarten again, following
Gail's lead, shuffling her feet, waving

her hands, singing along with Elvis,
"And he walks with me / And he talks with
me / And he tells me I am his own."

No Life Saving Measures

Driving home in a snow squall Lacy calls
from Winterberry and thinks Bobbi broke ribs,
maybe a hip too; Deb administered

morphine, which didn't touch her pain.
"I had to call 911," Lacy says, so I pull over
into a Dysart's Travel Stop, zero visibility;

Lacey apologizes knowing of all the right
answers this is not one I want to hear. "Your
mother is on her way to St. Joe's;

Deb's shift was over but she went with her
in the ambulance anyway; your mother was so
scaredconfusedinpain—all at once."

Do Not Hospitalize

"Good news," St. Joseph's
emergency room doctor says
synced with my truck's

speakers. "Your mother
is a miracle." And I want to
reach into the distance

between us—maybe fifty
miles since I'm in the Water-
ville area—and squeeze

the Hippocratic oath out of
her like you'd squeeze a tube
of mint toothpaste.

Stages of Dying

"Do you know what's going on?"
I ask Bobbi. "I think so," she answers,
chest heaving, fighting back wild

lupine tears, her left eye an ugly welt
from last week when she lost her balance
dressing in the bathroom. "Your mom

will fall, again," says the Hospice
nurse stethoscoping Bobbi's whooshing
heart murmur. "We come into this

life. We go out," Bobbi shudders,
unwraps a red striped peppermint candy,
sucks her lips: "What a shitty thing."

Respite Care

Auburn, the Hospice nurse,
hands me a business card;

"Call this number 24 hours
a day," she says. "We're

the emergency room now.
Your mother doesn't have to go

to St. Joe's anymore when
she falls or has pain."

Alzheimer's Apology Prayer

"I wish you were dead!" spewed out
of my mouth too easily as a teenager, but
I never wanted Bobbi dead. That's

what I am remembering now, sipping
coffee when, "I wish my mother would die,"
spewed again, decades later. This time,

to end her crying, I explain to my wife,
and shitting herself and the grief of losing
everything she has ever known.

Wondering Souls Live at the Memory Club

Ed from Hospice is recovering from a massive
stroke. "I'm in my seventies," he says, tuning a guitar,
words warped, nothing I would have noticed

if he didn't say something first; Ed grew up in Bar
Harbor, his father a biochemist at Jackson Lab. "Your
mom likes to sing with me," he says. "Do you want

to sing?" Ed takes Bobbi's hand; she appears confused
yet delighted for the attention. "God will take care of you,"
his tone is clear, resonant, solemn, and he smiles at

Bobbi bebopping her head. When Ed finishes, he asks
if it's ok to pray together before he leaves; Bobbi doesn't
say yes or no, so I nod my approval even though

my mother doesn't pray or think about God. After
reciting the "Lord's Prayer," Ed says, Amen, as if he is
teaching her a new word, but Bobbi is singing

along with Jerri now who is dancing the lindy hop
in a chair at the next table, arms, hands, and legs belting
out the iconic Andrew Sisters, World War II hit,

"Boogie Woogie Bugle Boy," Bluetoothed over a
flock of wireless speakers where church is the higher
power of any distraction, any fleeting relief.

Funeral Rites

In August, when Dr. Singer recommends
anti-psychotic drugs, I know it's time to make
funeral arrangements, figuratively bury

my mother, who never trusted doctors, who
died in a bloody, gangland-style slaying—suspect
walks up, suspect unloads a Glock of bullets

into her head, suspect flees on foot, gets away
as I listen to Dr. Singer's instructions and agree
to fill the prescriptions as soon as possible.

Taphophobia

"Dr. Singer has incredible radar,"
replies Susan during Bobbi's telephone
assessment. "If he thinks your mother

has two or three months to live, I'd
say he's probably close." Drawing dollar
sign doodles on my notes, my fingers

are heavy as headstones. Bobbi stays
at Winterberry Heights until she's dead
or moves to Dirigo Pines until she's

dead. The weight of this final decision,
while Susan stresses my role as Bobbi's
financial steward, buries me alive.

No Do-Overs

Tee helps me gather Bobbi's hooded jacket,
gloves, hat, cozy socks, boots—should she survive another
winter—bathroom basics, *nothing sharp*, we were told,
plus underclothes and photos of her dogs, total strangers
to her now. Tee was

in the Army before working here, and says she
had a difficult time adjusting, not the 12 hour shifts, the
emotional strain, the extra worry and love required
that nobody mentioned during the brief interview, but
like anything else, she

rolls her eyes, you adjust; Tee places the pink laundry
basket of towels and mismatched sheets on the cart, a grim
imbalance of what Bobbi has left after 82 years.
"Are you really sure this is all you're keeping? For your
mother?" "Yup," I reply,

scanning the disheveled room, flat screen tv, plastic
bougainvillea vines, camo toiletry bag, kitchen supplies and
luggage she'll never use again. Tee is in her 20s, but
Bobbi is as good as cremation ash. "The rest is garbage
or going to Goodwill."

Magic Eight Ball

Dr. Singer reviews Bobbi's final treatment
plan: Stop BuSpar, Stop Namenda. Stop Sertraline.
"Your mother doesn't need these medications

anymore." Then he sizes Bobbi up, and says,
"She probably has two or three months left," and
I picture Dr. Singer as Zoltar, a gypsy robot

in a fortune telling machine, turban, purple vest,
gawdy costume jewelry, crystal ball. Bobbi shrugs,
her face as blank and futureless as a corpse.

Born Again

Heading down the hallway for Bobbi's apartment we backtrack
to the tv room where Dr. Carroll flips through patient files. "Oh,
good morning," she waves, walks over. We discuss the stitches in
Bobbi's pinkie, I mention how she had a rough time with the staff
nurse at Winterberry, and Dr. Carroll scribbles in her pad

to contact Auburn for assistance, a Hospice nurse, who has
emergency room experience and can handle any old lady or Sas-
quatch. "I examined your mother last week," Dr. Carroll adds,
reaches out to pet robot-Max on his crusty snout. "There's no real
change since my previous visit. We are really just waiting,

now," she looks up, eyes as sad as the longest good-bye. I thank
Dr. Carroll for the updates, point Bobbi like a loaded gun in the
direction of room 244. Walking away my bones are rebar; then
cement fills me, every step a trial of errors, and I think, *Bobbi is
waiting for the miracle of her first son to call or visit.*

Compassionate Caring

"Let's speak Ukraine," I suggest
while sitting on Bobbi's bed holding
her fragile hand, blue and yellow

veins like Google Maps, one foot
in this world, the other in a new city,
another life. When she was a girl,

Bobbi spoke Ukrainian with her
mother, a private language of melody
and connection. "Blah, blah, blah,"

I singsong in my best Slavic accent,
how I've always spoken my mother's
mother tongue, so she laughs like

an explosion of paper confetti, then
she is unconscious again. Hospice says
Bobbi's organs are shutting down.

Wonder Woman

Sheila from Beacon Hospice sticks her head around
the corner. "Come in," Bobbi's voice is small. "I'm still
here." "You're an amazing woman," Sheila squeezes

Bobbi's feet over the covers; then both legs; then
a twig of a shoulder poking out from under the blanket;
and then Sheila's lips land on Bobbi's forehead. "If

I cracked my head like you, honey," Sheila pulls a
blouse off a hanger from the closet, "I'd be in traction!"
Sheila glances at Debby, Bobbi's caseworker, and

raises her eyebrows at the miracle of walking away
from St. Joe's emergency room after falling down a flight
of stairs. "How do you feel?" "Not all that amazing,"

Bobbi turns, looks at me reclined on the motorized lift
chair by the bed. "Maybe that's key in life, not knowing
how amazing we are," I joke but I am deadly serious.

Family Affair

Aunt Shirley texts,
Mom keeps asking for
Jennifer's phone

number. If you have
it please forward to me
and I'll remind her

to check in with
her grandma before
it's too late.

Fit as a Fiddle

Bobbi is a sack of complaints
ignoring death under a Pepsi Blue
sheet. Deb from Hospice takes

her twisted, arthritic fingers, rests
them in hers, fits the blood pressure
monitor around her skeletal wrist,

then presses the start button.
Once Deb is done examining Bobbi,
she looks at me, jazz-hands her

shapely breasts and thighs and
belly rolls, rolls her eyes, and says,
"Her *vitals* are better than mine."

Helpless

Sitting on the toilet Bobbi unravels
the roll of toilet paper from the dispenser,
eyes glassy, not seeing, mumbling

about her mother. "She's been talking
nonsense for a couple days," says Berg
lifting her. "What's holding you back,

Mom?" I ask once she is settled in bed,
again, her screams faded from the room
but not gone from my head. "I don't

know if I'll be happy or not," she slurs,
feet swimming from the excruciating pain
of her organs shutting down.

Dying Room

"Come sit by me," Bobbi croaks,
pats the side of her bed, so I move the chair
closer, slipping off my shoes, and I put up
my feet. "Are you mad?" she lifts

her head from the pillow, then back
down. "I never wanted trouble." "Of course
not, Mom," I reply, glance at the window;
the heavy curtain blocks the sun

from spilling in the room. This is the opposite
of a baby born, this is every son and his mother
being dead, the poignant scene in *Cool Hand
Luke* where Luke's mother,

frail and propped in the back of a pickup
truck, visits him in prison to reminisce before
she dies. A sad scene but necessary. "Why
did you leave us?" Bobbi's tongue falls

out of her mouth, pokes dry lips; she thinks
I'm her first husband, my father. "Something
was calling," I reply. "Something good,
I hope," Bobbi's eyes drift.

Sunset at the Bitter End

"If you don't wake up tomorrow,
are you ready to meet God?" Chaplin
Gail sits crouched beside Bobbi,

rubbing her arm, skin like shriveled
peaches, and Bobbi's reply, "Oh, that's
a big one," reminds me of Betsy, a

neighbor whose dying mother, who
lived out-of-state, would not let life go
until she and her daughter said their

final goodbyes. If Bobbi is waiting
for anybody, it's my brother, her first
son, handicapped his entire life by

drugs and despair. "Are you worried
about Jerry?" Chaplin Gail finger brushes
silver cowlicks from Bobbi's eyes.

Direct Cremation II

"I don't know how
to have this conversation,"
I say over and over

in my head when I
call the funeral director
and the phone rings

and rings until I don't
leave a message until I call
back a third time.

Ecclesiastes 1:9

"Oh, love finds," says Bobbi sipping hot chocolate,
and her face contorts, flawless, momentary delight
as if making no sense anymore doesn't matter as much
as sugar on your tongue or playing dolls with
Frances. "Baby," Frances gives me

her infant, who is dressed in a pink onesie, her hair
magic-markered and fading; Frances doesn't make
any more sense than Bobbi when she talks, so I pretend
with them both, "Does this tickle?" I poke Baby
but look at Frances. "Oh, love finds,"

says Bobbi pulling the doll from me, one arm
supporting its head, the other supporting its
bottom like she cradled her first son over sixty years
ago, and her face contorts, flawless, momentary
delight as if making no sense anymore

doesn't matter as much as the tender potential of
love in whatever form it takes. "Give Frances
her baby back, now, Mom," I say after seeing heartache
on Frances's face, and when I pry the doll from her
hands, I think of the coloring book pages on

Bobbi's bedside table that Gail, the hospice chaplain,
brought as a spiritual activity to work on during
her last visit. Flipping pages a set of drawings portrayed
the arch of life as line-art—a newborn swaddled
in a blanket that Bobbi colored blue who

ages into a toddler who ages into a teen who ages
into a college graduate who ages into a first time
parent and then into midlife and finally old-age, a shrunken
woman hunched over the caption, "What has been
will be again, / what has been done

will be done again; / there is nothing new under the
sun." Bobbi tried to color the old woman using
a purple crayon but instead the old woman, struggling to
regain her place in the world, is crossed-out, broad,
frustrated strokes.

Buffalo Plaid

Polar fleece scarf half hitched
around Bobbi's neck she snoozes
slumped in a chair. "Got to get
out of here,"

she mumbles tapping her feet
and rubbing her leg, eyes closed.
"I don't know what's going
on," she drums,

keeping time with pink painted
fingernails. "What are you listening
to?" I say when she opens her
heavy, dark marble

eyes. "Huh?" Bobbi replies,
shakes off a confusion. "Your feet
are dancing," I point. "What song
is playing in your

head?" Bobbi squints as if I'm
only as real as her memories which
are blurry and says, "Who wants
to be dead!"

Strange Brew

By the eighth ring the phone's ringing blends
into one sound, bending with the humming of the
electric wall heater blowing hot, dry air

into the apartment. Bobbi is adrift, half asleep
on her side, hugging a robot goldendoodle. "What
is that noise?" she says to Max, who woofs

a small, slurred bark because his batteries are
low. What quality of life remains when nothing
is familiar anymore, the phone ringing, a

mechanical dog that's not your dog, breakfast
from supper, your son's green eyes? "Bobbi, I can
help you answer your phone," says Amber

Bobbi's favorite resident-assistant who heard
the phone ringing from the hallway. "Who the hell
are you?" says Bobbi. "And what are you doing

in my room?" Amber has seen this final letting
go of memory too many times before, a slop sink
half filled with water spilling down the drain.

Purgatory

"You've had a good life,
Mom; you've given me poetry,
stories, and reasons to

dream; I need nothing,
so be done, now; stop hurting,
stop waiting, dead will be

gentler," I try to sound
convincing while she lies in bed,
not living, not dying either.

Drinking Chocolate

Too sedated to drink or eat on her own
I ask a resident assistant if I can give Bobbi's
hot chocolate to Alice, sitting in a

wheelchair at the table with us, flipping
pages in a back issue of *Maine Home + Design*
and talking to herself as if she's dining with

family and friends. "This is so good," she
says before she ever sips it, but then she sips
it, and her eyes are clear for an instant.

Matricide

Nero ordered the murder of his mother;
Queen Amastris of Heraclea was drowned
by her two sons; Cleopatra III of Egypt

was assassinated by order of her son; Ptolemy
had his wife murdered—she was his stepmother;
Mary Ann Lamb killed her invalid mother

during a mental break-down; Sidney Harry
Fox killed his mother for her life insurance;
during the Battle of Okinawa, civilians

killed their mothers to prevent them from
being raped and killed by American forces;
Henry Lee Lucas stabbed his mother

in the neck, killing her; Charles Whitman
shot his mother before going on a killing spree;
serial killer Edmund Kemper beat his mother

to death; Bradford Bishop beat his mother to
death too; Jim Gordon, drummer for Derek and
the Dominos, stabbed his mother to death

with a butcher's knife; Antony Baekeland
murdered his mother at their luxurious London
flat because she forced him to have sex

with her to cure his homosexuality; 1950's,
Hollywood actress Susan Cabot was beaten to
death by her son, Timothy Roman; 15 year

old Brett Reider from Omaha stabbed his
mother to death; Peter Lundin, 19 year's old,
choked his mother to death; Aaron Brown

16 years old, blew his mother's face off with
a shotgun; Michael Kenneth, the Geneva County
murderer shot his mother first, then her dogs;

identical twins Jasmiyah and Tasmiyah
Whitehead murdered their mother, Nikki; Dr.
I. Kathleen Hagen, a prominent urologist,

asphyxiated her mother; Yukio Yamaji killed
his mother with a baseball bat; Adam Lanza, the
Sandy Hook Elementary School shooter, shot

and killed his mother; Orestes murdered his
mother, plunged a dagger in her chest up to its
cross-guard, and the Furies hunted him until

he went mad; Aunt Shirley texts about how I'm
earning Angel's wings caretaking for my mother;
I need therapy, I text back, *not salvation*.

III: NO MORE LONG-TERM

Disorder of Events

"How's your mother?" Keith asks
while we walk to the ferry. Keith's mom
is starting to lose track of herself

like Bobbi, so I don't want to give
the standard, she's fine, she's tough reply,
but my heart is sore, rubbed raw

from waiting. Like 20 questions
Alzheimer's disease is a waiting game.
"I'm headed to Florida next week

to see mine," he adds, the double tax
of caring stamped into his face. "Bobbi died
months ago, Keith, back in April."

I look him in the eyes, so he knows
I'm dead serious. "I'm just waiting for her
to take that last, big breath."

The Mathematics of Understanding

Imagine looking in the mirror and seeing
your brain deteriorate as a time-lapse video,
blue, showy hydrangea flowers, Bobbi's

favorite, wilting on their stems before your
eyes, seeing a lifetime wilt away. Bedbound
Bobbi counts to nine under her breath,

stops, then starts from one again until I
interrupt with how my marinara never tastes
as good as hers. One, two, three, four, five,

six, seven, eight, nine numbers show order
and proof of identity. "I don't know why she
counts," Rex, the hospice nurse, shrugs.

Little Birdie

Bobbi opens her mouth, breath funky
like CBD oil. "It's Gary, Mom. I'm still here."
Then I rub her throat with the back of three

fingers, her skin softer than it looks, like worn,
broken-in leather boots. "Swallow, first," I whisper
in a teary voice. I promised nobody would feed

her like an infant or invalid. Breaking that
promise, ambient flute rhythms chirping on the
radio, I spoon a smidgen more of applesauce.

Separation

"Are you done with this
world?" I ask. "Uh-huh," Bobbi
replies, zero resistance.

Tradition

"Do you have pickled herring for tonight?"
I ask my mother the year she turned 80. "Oh,
no, dammit, I forgot, again," she sighs into

the phone. "Well, Walmart had Blue Hill Bay
herring in dill marinade that I can't wait to try,"
and then I read the jar's ingredients. "When

I was growing up in New Cassel," Bobbi
reflects, "Grandma would buy whole herrings,
smoked ones, every New Year's Eve, and

we'd pick off them for days. For luck. Maybe
next year you'll remind me," she laughs. "Your
mother can use all the luck she can get now."

Look Away

"There are things
I don't want to know."
"What things,

Mom?" "Dementia."
"Then you don't have
to know." "Okay."

"I'll call back, Mom,
after work." "It's late,
let's talk in the

morning, Honey." *It
is morning, Mom,* but
I don't correct her.

Pleasantly Demented

"Tinkle, tinkle, in the grass,
vaffanculo, and kiss my ass,"
Bobbi makes a clown face

and belly laughs walking
Max, her toy poodle. Today's
humidity is thick, heat index

ninety-two percent cicadas,
an ear piercing noise, as if car
alarms are tripped all over

the senior golf community.
"My mother, the gangsta rappa,"
I laugh too. "Was that a beat

from Nicki Minaj or a PSA
you stole watching Fox News?"
"Inspiration," Bobbi double

high-fives her reply, Publix
grocery bag in a fist above her
head. For a flash she is Sonja,

Viking warrior queen, shrill
sword ready for battle, blood,
mayhem, and then she is

Bobbi, again, 80 years old,
thin white hair that used to be
red, her face wrinkled, her

mouth puckered; without teeth
she is shriveled, ten years older.
Max squats in the swamp

grass and a golf cart whizzes
by driving on the wrong side of
Fairway Boulevard. "Such a

good boy, my Max," Bobbi
praises the poodle but ignores
the golfers. "I love this dog,

like a son," Bobbi stargazes,
and I gawk at the grocery bag
dangling in her bent arthritic

fingers. I shake my head,
"I told you, never the dog shit.
I'll paint your condo pink

flamingo, but Max's turds
are yours, not mine." "Please!"
Bobbi barks. "Please, help

your mother. You know my
damn knees don't bend!" Then
Bobbi's face is empty, as if

she materialized from another
planet and can't figure out why
she's crouching like a garden

gnome in the neighbor's front
lawn. "Max, stop pulling!" she
stands, wobbles, then granny

knots the grocery bag. "Hold
this, dammit," Bobbi's voice is
flat, alien. "No way," I reply

thinking about what I read
Googling dementia: *Treat your
mother like an adult, not a*

*child as her abilities decrease
and her needs increase.* "You'll
get yours, Mister. Paybacks!"

Bobbi's smirk is back, full of
screws. Up ahead a woman cuts
across the palm-leaf littered

green. "Good morning, Jean,"
Bobbi calls out, yanking Max's
leash, and he double-takes

spotting Stuart, a Shih Tzu,
cute and jittery, nose tracking
the news weather helicopter

circling overhead. "Is this
one of your sons?" Jean points
and cigarette smoke engulfs

us. "My baby," Bobbi scoffs,
"who doesn't think I know my
ass from a hole-in-the-wall

anymore." "The nerve!" tugs
Jean, but Bobbi is stalled again,
like the black, rusty-bucket

Nova she drove in the 1970s
after my father left. "*And* don't
say Hurricane Irma if *he's*

in the building," Bobbi adds
once the bedlam in her brain re-
routes. "Don't," Jean shrugs.

"Seven Springs is hurricane
proof." "That's what I've been
telling him," Bobbi swipes

swaths of smoke, then shifts
the subject: "Since when do you
smoke?" "Oh since forever,"

Jean puffs, gray-minty rings
curling up into blue, spiked hair,
Max and Stuart sniffing each

other in spazzy circles, cicadas
screeching, and a blast of sirens
mix with the sun and clouds

gathering up the sky. "Max,
stop it!" Bobbi spins, untangles
the dogs, huffs and puffs, and

fusses with the zipper-pull
on her fanny pack. "Where did
you get this dog?" Bobbi

takes out teeth, pops them in
her mouth. "What a beauty like
my Max." Jean looks at me;

I look at Jean. Bobbi has that
doomed, brainsick-look again.
You can fight getting old;

you can get out of bed each
day, get dressed, drink coffee,
walk your dog, even pick up

his shit, but if high-winds roll
in, you can't outrun or disguise
dementia with plastic bags

from the supermarket. "We,
should really get going," I say
snatching the bag of poop.

"Fingers crossed the airport
in Clearwater doesn't shutdown
too." "Nice to finally meet

you," Jean crosses her fingers.
"This is my youngest son from
Maine," Bobbi smiles but

teeth fly out of her mouth and
into a fist of tissues, Category 5,
crushing wind, catastrophic

surges, flooding, memory care,
hospice, the strongest hurricane
on record in the Sea of Atlas.

Crying for Help

"Killing hurts," a song from the 1990s
by Helmet, loops in my head when silver
tears like an SOS fall from Bobbi's

clouded eyes; she is flipped on her side
being changed, arms limp like a cadaver's
arms. Decent ways to die are painless

and peaceful. A bad death is any trauma,
any violence or despair. Not being able to
express yourself is torment. "My mom

is suffering," I speed dial hospice, plead
for mercy and enough morphine to choke a
horse, one of Bobbi's pet expressions.

United Health Care

"What's your plan, Mom?" I ask, "if Jimmy dies
before you?" "He's fine," she replies as if he wasn't
at the hospital yesterday, shrill pain in his chest

again while playing golf with his sons. "I called
Parker Ridge anyway. The senior community in Blue
Hill that I mentioned." "Jimmy's not dead yet," she

snaps. "If you live closer, I can help you once he
is. Take you to the doctor. The grocery store. Anything
you need." "I don't need help!" she barks into the

phone. "Then what's your plan, Mom? What's
your long-term plan when you're all alone?" "911!"
she yells. "There is no plan, no more long-term!"

So Be It

"On three," says John, the funeral attendant,
who drove from Fort Kent to pick up Bobbi's empty

vehicle, and we lift her onto the gurney,
and into a body-bag. "May she embrace God

and find peace," hospice nurse Laura asked if we
could pray, not knowing if prayer is how I say

thanks or seek comfort. "Amen," I whisper expecting
my response to sound dishonest, but it doesn't.

Gently Down the Stream

"Row, row, row your boat,"
Bobbi and I sing another round,
laughing, loving every twisted

syllable. I am eight or fifty
two years old. We are stopped
at the busy traffic light at

Newbridge Road and Hempstead
Turnpike. When red turns to green,
Mom's rust-bucket Chevy Nova

stalls. Popping gears on the
steering column into park, she
pumps the gas. Grinds

the ignition. Both of us belting
offkey, "Merrily, merrily, merrily,
merrily. Life is but a *giffft.*"

About the Author

Gary Rainford, author of *Salty Liquor* and *Liner Notes*, lives year-round on Swan's Island with his wife and daughter. Gary is a storyteller who uses poetry to tell stories. Connect with Gary at www.garyrainford.com.

CPSIA information can be obtained
at www.ICGtesting.com
Printed in the USA
BVHW011208300822
645842BV00009B/676